THE
STILL MIND
PRESENT MOMENT
OPEN HEART

by Daniel R. Condron
D.M., D.D., M.S.

SOM Publishing
Windyville, Missouri 65783

Library of Congress Control Number: 2008929911

Library of Congress Cataloging in Publication Data
Condron, Daniel R.
  The **Still Mind, Present Moment, Open Heart**
  Summary: A new Holy Scripture for the world that
explains the True Nature of Reality and how to live in
harmony with that Reality.

ISBN: 0-944396-43-1
EAN: 978-0-944386-43-9

© July, 2008   School of Metaphysics No. 100193
PRINTED IN THE UNITED STATES OF AMERICA

If you desire to learn more about the research and teachings in this
book, write to:

School of Metaphysics Headquarters
163 Moon Valley Road
Windyville, Missouri 65783

Or call us at (417) 345-8411
Visit us on the internet at:
www.som.org
www.dreamschool.org

Table of Contents

Introduction

After 25 years of meditation I achieved a Still Mind.

After 26 years of meditation I achieved the Present Moment.

After 27 years of meditation, service and teaching, I gained or received the Open Heart.

From this came a greater need and inner urge to help and aid humanity.

World peace can only be achieved when people are at peace within themselves. People can only be at peace within themselves when there is enough mental self-discipline to cause the mind to be still.

A scattered mind can never know peace.

A busy brain can never experience peace.

Only the Still Mind in the Present Moment can know peace. Mental discipline must be practiced daily in order for the Still Mind to be achieved. Mental discipline may be practiced through the art and science of meditation, concentration, visualization and imaging, breath-work-life-force exercises, and memory exercises. Of these, meditation is the most important. To successfully meditate one must be able to concentrate. Therefore, concentration is a necessary prerequisite for meditation.

Most people live out their lives for what is temporary. Most people give the temporary this highest priority.

The permanent and lasting is not easily seen or perceived by the five physical senses of sight, smell, taste, touch, and hearing. This is because the sense organs themselves are of the temporary.

I was once asked the following question by a friend who happens to be a Baptist minister, "What do you do with eternity?" meaning how do I explain that concept. At the time I did not give him what I thought to be an acceptable answer. So I stilled my mind and over time I received the answer. A few months later when I saw my friend, I reminded him of his question about eternity. He remembered the question. I said, "Eternity is in the Present Moment." To which he replied, "Well that makes sense. Jesus said, 'The kingdom of Heaven is at hand'."

The present moment affords the answer to most problems and questions because the present moment offers truth. A still mind is required to know the present moment and mental discipline is required to develop a still mind. This is why most people do not have a still mind. Not having a still mind, their attention jumps from imperfect memories of the past to fantasies about an imagined future, or else the attention jumps to whatever grabs their attention in the outer environment.

A billboard along the highway, a magazine ad, beautiful scenery, a loud noise, something unusual, anything that is different from the norm, seems to capture the attention.

So what we have is a world full of busy brains mostly controlled by the ego. The ego is the physical body semi-intelligence controlling or overriding the Real Self that is I AM. When human consciousness is identified with the physical body and engrossed in the five physical senses, and therefore physical limitations, then does the ego take hold. The ego does not reason. Although its logic is subtle and cunning, the ego does not accept thought as cause. Therefore, the ego identified person blames the environment for one's troubles. The soul or I AM identified being, however, understanding one's thoughts as the cause of one's life, circumstances and experiences, accepts responsibility for one's life as it is. Accepting this responsibility, such a one constantly strives to upgrade and update thought in order to advance the Self mentally, emotionally, and physically.

Thought is Cause is a Universal Truth. The mind disciplined one accepts this as fact and knows this to be true. The ego-centered person does not accept thought is cause as truth and therefore fears the environment as the controller of the Self. Therefore, the discipline minded one living in truth is able to master the Self and by this to influence the environment productively.

The still mind enables conscious choice.
The busy brain leads to habitual re-action.

All great progress in humanity's condition is brought about by individuals who have become great through discipline of the mind and Self.

The still mind brings one into the present moment. By this, I mean the disciplined one who gains the still mind stops being engrossed in brain memories of a supposed past.

Brain memories when dwelt upon tend to place a false perception over the present moment. For example, a person who wears green-colored sunglasses sees the world as having a green tint. This colorized perception is askew from the reality the naked eyes alone perceive.

So it is with habitual memory images. The color, flavor, form or shape that one is habitually pre-dispositioned to, always colorizes or filters the present experience. For example, a habitually angry person finds reasons for justifying being continually angry in different situations and circumstances with different people and places all the while justifying such outrageous behavior. The perpetually sad person finds reasons for being perpetually sad. The person of low self-worth finds excuses to over and over convince others of his or her worthlessness.

The disciplined visionary realizes a duty to all mankind. Such a one going deep within in meditation, realizes the true nature and value of the Superconscious Self.

The disciplined one, correctly perceiving the present moment, realizes the unique and immense opportunity in every moment.

Every moment is different.

The still minded one realizes the truth of this. Each moment affords a unique opportunity for advancement and betterment on all levels.

The habitual one with scattered, undisciplined thoughts views each circumstance, situation and place with the same limitation.

Believing these self-imposed limitations to be truth, the undisciplined person doesn't even believe it is possible to improve the situations or circumstances of the life.

Therefore, in order to help each individual lead a better, greater life and for the betterment of the entire planet, it is imperative that each person learn to discipline and still the restless thoughts of the mind.

World peace begins with peace in each person's mind. We sometimes call this Peace of Mind. Undisciplined, out of control thoughts and re-actions can never be peaceful nor can they bring about peace of mind. Only the disciplined and still mind can bring about peace.

In the year 2006, I wrote the **The Emptiness Sutra**. I wrote this book spontaneously after sitting for two hours in still mind meditation with the class I was teaching.

After achieving the still mind, I realized a need to teach what I had learned, achieved and received. Therefore I created the Still Mind Class which I teach at the College of Metaphysics. In the Still Mind Class which meets monthly, we sit in still-minded meditation for two hours to begin the class. At the end of the second class, I asked everyone to write down what they experienced during the 2-hour still mind meditation.

I also, then, began to write my experience. I wrote spontaneously for quite some time until looking up I noticed all the students were finished writing so I stopped also. Then I taught the rest of class.

Later that same day after the class was over, I felt an inner urge to write more. It felt like I wasn't done or complete with my writing. So I sat down and wrote. I wrote spontaneously until I was done. The result is **The Emptiness Sutra**. This book flowed effortlessly through me without change. It came from alignment of conscious and subconscious minds and attunement to Superconscious mind.

The opening to higher consciousness that I experienced in an infancy stage two years ago has now matured into an adulthood of high consciousness state and therefore I present this book **The Still Mind, Present Moment, Open Heart**. This book was written over the course of several days. I caused my conscious and subconscious minds to align and to attune to superconscious mind. Then from this state of high consciousness I brought forth this book. It has not been changed but is exactly as I wrote it down on paper as it came to me.

In **The Still Mind, Present Moment, Open Heart** is the hope of the world for we must learn to not only **do** but also to **be**. Humanity must learn the art and science of being.

The power is in the Present Moment.

Now is all I have.

Now is all you have.

Now, the Present Moment, is all we have.

We are here to help life and humanity.

It is never too late to do the right thing.

It is the right or correct thing to be in the Present Moment.

The Present Moment is all we have. Therefore, seize the moment, and use it to the fullest to benefit Self and others.

One time I said to myself, "If there's not love in my life then it's not worth living."

Once you achieve the Still Mind and move more and more into the Present Moment, your heart will begin to open and you will discover a greater love than you have ever known before. Old, restrictive ways of thinking will fall away to make way for a new, greater you and a new, greater life.

Once the Open Heart is achieved all learning, knowledge, and understanding come pouring into your being at a quicker, greater and more expansive rate than ever before. Learning becomes easier and the life lessons become greater.

In the Still Mind, Present Moment, Open Heart are all the life lessons you will ever need! You will have the power to receive them and assimilate them.

You will exist in a state of high consciousness and being, knowing who you are, the purpose of life and how to fulfill your life's assignment.

In the Still Mind, Present Moment and Open Heart,

Daniel R. Condron

CHAPTER 1
THE STILL MIND

The Still Mind is of Utmost
Importance for all of Humanity.
Most People Think too Much.
They May Think They Are
Producing More by Thinking
More but Ultimately This Brings
Collapse of One's Mental,
Emotional or Physical Health.

The Mind, as it is Designed,
is to Be Consciously Used.
Every Consciously Chosen Thought
that is Spoken Aloud to Others
is an Effort to Use the
Conscious Mind.

Every Scattered or Habitual
Thought is a Brain Thought.

The Brain is a Physical Organ
of the Physical Body.
The Mind is to Be Used to
Direct the Brain.
The Self is to Direct the Mind.

Only Mental Discipline Brings About
the Productive and Conscious
Use of the Mind.

The Highest Use of the Mind is to
Know the Self. The Mind is the Vehicle
to Know the Self. To Know the Self is
Eternal and Permanent and Real.

To Live the Life Engrossed in
Sensory Experience and the Brain
is to Live the Life for the temporary.

To Misuse the Mind to only
Accumulate Greater Physical
Possessions Causes One to Miss
the True Purpose of Life.
To Know the Purpose of Life
One Must Employ the Mind
as the Servant of the Self to
Know the Self.
What is the Relation of the
Still Mind to Using the Mind
to Know the Self?

The One Who Practices Concentration
and Meditation Gradually or Quickly
Comes to Slow the Thoughts Down and
Achieves Greater and Greater Spaces
Between the Thoughts.
After Awhile the Space is So Great
Between the Thoughts That One
Realizes Thoughts Can be Consciously
Chosen Instead of Just Having Them
Pop Randomly into One's Mind.

In the Prolonged Spaces
Between One's Thoughts
One Discovers the Ability to
Consciously Choose Thoughts.

This Is the Beginning of the
Waking Up Process.

To Be Awake One Must
Consciously Choose Thoughts.
Only a Consciously Awake
Being Can Fulfill the
Highest and
True Purpose of Life.

In the Space Between Thoughts
Exists an Opportunity for
Wakefulness and Conscious
Choice of Thought.
The Busy, Habitual Brain that
Rapidly Thinks Many Thoughts
Can Never Know the
Power of the Mind or
the Real Self.

The Still Mind is the Beginning of
All Creation and Stillness is the
End of All Creation.

The One Who Causes the Mind
to be Still is a Conscious Creator.
Such a One Consciously
Creates Thought.
Only the Still Minded
One Knows Creation.

When the Mind Becomes
Disciplined and Focused the
Scattering of the Attention is
Diminished. Then the Duration of
the Attention on One Point of Focus
Increases. This is Known as Concentration
and Leads to the
Discipline of the Mind.

Mental Discipline is the Foundation
and First Key for Knowing Self,
Creation and All of Mind.

This Increase in the Duration of the
Attention on One Point of Focus
Brought About by Conscious Choice
Leads to the Realization of Power.
This is the Beginning of Freedom.

The Still Mind Is Needed.

The Still Mind Is Needed in
Order for Freedom to Occur.

The Still Mind Is Needed for
Awareness to Occur.

The Still Mind Is Needed for
Understanding to Occur.

The Still Mind Is Needed in Order to
Receive the High Knowledge.

The One of Strong Mind Knows
the Still Mind.

The One of Powerful Mind

Knows the Still Mind.

The One Who Goes Beyond Mind
Knows the Stillness That Is the
Source Point of Creation.

The Still Mind Is Needed for
the Highest Love.

The Still Mind Is Needed to
Know the Present Moment.

The Still Mind Is Needed

to Know Time.

The Still Mind Is Needed to
Know Time, Physical Time,
as an Illusion.

The Still Minded One

Knows Duration.

The Still Minded One

Knows Self.

The Still Minded One

Cares for Others.

In the Still Mind

Consciousness Expands to Infinity.

Then the Still Minded One

Experiences the Urge to Uplift

the Consciousness of All

Humanity Which is to Save

Humankind.

In the Still Mind One Knows

Connectedness.

All True Power Comes From
a Still Mind.

———

The One With a Still Mind

Knows Love.

———

———————

The Still Minded One
Knows Peace.

———————

Only the One of the Still Mind

Knows Peace.

The One With a Still Mind

Knows the Quietness.

The One With a Still Mind

Knows the Silence.

The One With a Still Mind

Knows the Quiet Self.

The Higher the Consciousness,
the Quieter the Mind.
The Quieter the Mind the
More the High Consciousness
Becomes Available.
The Still Minded One Knows
the High Consciousness.

The Still Minded One

Knows Time.

The Still Minded One

Knows Connectedness.

The Still Minded One Knows the
True Nature of Reality.
The Still Minded One Knows the
Joy of the Present Moment.
The Still Minded One
Experiences Bliss.

Where Is the Still Mind?
In the Space Between
One's Thoughts.
The Space Between Thoughts
Has to Be Extended in Order
to Have Enough Awareness
to Know the Space.

When the Effort to Habitually
produce One Thought
after Another Ceases Then
Space Begins.

In Space Is the Energetic
Power of Love.

In the Space One Can

Know Truth.

In the Space One Can

Receive Light.

In the Space One Can
Know Life.
In the Space there
Is Room Enough To Live.
In the Space there Is
Infinite Room.

In the Space there
Is Caring.

In the Space the
Interconnectedness of
All Beings Is Known.
In Space the True Nature
of Reality that Is
Connectedness
Is Known.

In Space, Separation Is Seen to
Be the Grand Illusion.

———————

The One of the Still Mind
Knows Space.
The One of the Still Mind
Knows Openness.
Because the Stilled Minded
One is Open, Such a One
Receives and Knows Space.

———————

———————

This Is the
Highest Teaching.

———————

———————

Let Those Who Would Know,
Prepare Themselves to Receive.

Discipline of the Mind Is
the Foundation for Knowing
the Still Mind.

For the One of a Still Mind,

Each Moment Is Different.

Each Experience Is Different.

All of Physical Life Changes.
Just as a Fire Changes and
Transforms what It Burns,
Reducing It to its
Elemental Particles,
So Does Physical Life
Transform from Structured
Form to Elemental Particles.

All Physical Life Is Either
Being Created or Decaying.
Therefore, Still the Mind and
Use the Present Moment
to the Fullest.

To Use the Present Moment
to the Fullest Is to Receive
the Essence of the Permanent
and Eternal Learning from
the Temporary Situation
created by Temporary Forms.
Glean the Permanent from
the Temporary.

Love and Truth are Permanent.

All Physical Forms are Temporary.

Stones are Temporary.

———————

The Still Mind Perceives the
Real from the Unreal.

The Still Minded One
Knows the Permanent.
The Still Minded One
Knows the Permanent
in the Space.

CHAPTER 2
THE PRESENT MOMENT

Once the Mind Becomes Still
the Present Moment Is
Discovered.

There Is No Future.

There Is No Past.

There Is Only the

Eternal Now.

Therefore, One Who Dwells in
Partial Memories of the Past that
Have Been Stored in the Brain
Lives in an Illusion.
One Who Constantly Fantasizes
about the Imagined Future
also Does Not Consciously Exist
in the True Reality.

The Enlightened Ones Always
Exist in the Ever Present,
Eternal Now, the True Reality.

The More Enlightened
One Becomes,
the More One Has
the Attention
in the Present Moment.

How Can One Be Truly Alive
While Trying to Exist in a
Brain Memory of the Past?

Only the Present Moment

Offers the Opportunity

for Enlightenment.

Only the Present Moment

Offers the Opportunity

to Know the Self.

Only the Present Moment
Offers the Opportunity to Be
in the Mind and Overcome
Entrapment in the Brain
and Engrossment in
Sensory Experiences.

The Enlightened One Is Awake
in the Present Moment.

What Is the

Present Moment?

The Present Moment Is
the True Reality.
I AM--
is in the Present Moment.
I Was--
is a Physical, Partial Brain
Memory of the Past.
I Will Be--
is a Fantasized Future.

Why Is it People Do Not
Know the Present Moment?
People Do Not Know
the Present Moment
Because They Do Not
Discipline Their Minds.

The Mind is the Vehicle to
Know the Self and
the True Reality.
Mental Discipline of the Mind
Is the Key to Mastering the Mind
in Order That it May Serve
as a Conscious Vehicle
for the Self.

A Conscious Choice

Made

in the Present Moment

Affords

Infinite Possibilities.

A Conscious Thought
Imaged in the Present Moment
Creates the Potential for
Infinite Manifestations.

The Present Moment
Affords the Opportunity
to Know Self
as Infinite Being.

The Present Moment Gives
Infinite Energy.

———

The Still Mind,
in the Present Moment,
Gives Infinite Intelligence.

Infinite Intelligence.

Infinite Energy.

Infinite Manifestation.

Infinite Being.

All Are Available in the

Present Moment.

What Is the Present Moment?
The Present Moment Is What IS.
The Present Moment Is the All.
The Present Moment Is the
True Reality.

In the Present Moment Exists the
Opportunity to Receive.
In the Present Moment Exists the
Opportunity to Give.
All That Exists Is Available in the
Present Moment.

———————

Fear Will Never Give One
the Present Moment.
Therefore, Fear Never
Brings Prosperity.

———————

All Great Progress
for Humanity Has
Occurred in the
Present Moment.

All Great Progress Has
Come From Those Who
Are in the Mind in the
Present Moment.

Those That Dwell in the
Fear Memories of a
Fantasized Past Never
Create Great Progress.

Those That Fantasize
about the future and
Never Take Action on
Their Thoughts Never Make Great
Progress.

The True Nature of Reality

Is Known in the Present Moment.

The One Who Has
Stilled the Mind to Live in the
Present Moment Knows
the True Nature of Reality as
Connectedness.

The One Who Lives in
Connectedness Is Capable
in Ways Others Are Not.
Such a One Has Power
Others Do Not.

The One Who Lives in the
Present Moment Finds
Peace in the Present Moment.

Only Those in the Present Moment
Know Peace for the Present Moment.
The True Reality and Peace are Only
Known in the Present Moment.

The Real Self Is Known

in the True Real-ity.

The Real Self Is Known
in the Present Moment.

Love, Light and Truth
are Known in the
Present Moment.

All Creation Is Made of
Light and Space.

Light Is Known in
the Present Moment.
Space Is Known in
the Present Moment.
Bliss Is Known in
the Present Moment.

All That Is Known Is Known

in the Present Moment.

The One Point of Focus

That Is Most Wanted and

Most Needed Is Love.

This Is the Key That Aligns

With the Galactic Core.

There Are Many Who Are

Aware of the Power of Love and

Many Who Want to Bring It and Many

Who Do Bring It.

Love Is the Energy of Space and

Within the Space the

Tension Dissipates.

This Is a Common Learning

For All of Humankind in the Present.

The Present Moment
affords the Opportunity
to Know Love.

The Present Moment
affords the Opportunity
to Give and Receive Love.

The Present Moment
Enables One to
Know Space.

The Present Moment

Enables One to

Know Love as the

Energy of Space.

In Those Who Live
in the Present Moment
conflict Is Resolved.

———

In Those Who Know
the Present Moment
Love Dissipates the
Tension of Conflict.

Love Is Known in the Space
of the Present Moment.

_____

In the Present Moment Is One

Attuned to the All.

In the Present Moment

One Knows

the Conscious Mind.

In the Present Moment

One Knows

the Subconscious Mind.

In the Present Moment

One Knows

the Superconscious Mind.

In the Present Moment

One Knows

I AM.

All That Is,

Exists in the

Present Moment.

The Christ Exists in the
Present Moment.
The Atman Exists in the
Present Moment.
The Buddha Exists in the
Present Moment.
All Live in the
Present Moment.

All That Lives,

Lives in the

Present Moment.

Plants Love the
Present Moment.

A Garden Loves

the Present Moment.

Kindness Is in the
Present Moment.
Tenderness Is in the
Present Moment.
Openness Is in the
Present Moment.

The Joy of Life Is in the
Present Moment.
The Purpose of Life Is in the
Present Moment.
Caring Is in the
Present Moment.
Understanding Is in the
Present Moment.

Why Wait for the
Future to Arrive?
Why Dwell on the
Past That Is Over?

The Present affords
Infinite Possibilities.
The Present Moment
affords Everything.

Anything One Wants to
Create for the Future Comes
From the Present Moment.
Anything That One Wants to
be Better Than the Past Comes
From the Present Moment.

All Peace, Love and Harmony

Come From

the Present Moment.

All Pain and Suffering From

the Past Is Released

in the Present Moment.

The Ability to Let Go of
Limitations Is Achieved
in the Present Moment.

Openness Is in the
Present Moment.

Why Do People Have
Their Attention in the
Past or Future Instead of the
Ever Present, Eternal, Now?
Because It Is Easier to Be in
the Brain Than in the Mind.
Mental Discipline is
Required to Command,
Wield, and Use the Mind.
Habitual Thinking Keeps
One Engrossed in the
Brain and Body.

The Mind Is the Vehicle
to Know the Self.
The Brain Is the Organ for
Surviving in the Physical Life.

Only the One Who Masters the Mind
Can Know the Real Self.
The Mind is Available in the Present
Moment.

CHAPTER 3
THE OPEN HEART

The Open Heart Reveals
the Way to the Real Self.
In the Open Heart One
Realizes the Permanent
Understanding of Self.

Until the Heart is Open
the Self Remains Closed Off to
and Oblivious of the Truth of Life.

The Open Heart Enables One
to Know the Sacred Heart.
In the Sacred Heart the Real Self Resides.

In the Open Heart Resides Truth.
In the Open Heart One
Experiences Love.
In the Open Heart One Knows
the True Meaning of Love.

The Open Heart Is the Doorway
to the Sacred Heart.

In the Sacred Heart Is Revealed

the True Meaning of Life.

In the Sacred Heart the

Highest Purpose of Life Is

Known to Be Love.

In the Open Heart

One Discovers

the True Nature of Reality.

In the Open Heart

One Knows

the True Nature of Reality.

In the Open Heart
One Discovers and Knows
the True Nature of Reality
as Connectedness.

In the Open Heart

One Discovers a Higher Meaning

and Purpose to Life.

The One That Has the Attention
in the Present Moment
Comes to Experience and Know
the Open Heart.

The Open Heart Enables

Conscious Connection

With Other Hearts.

The Open Heart Is Energetic.

The Open Heart Is Alive.

The Open Heart Is Connected.

The Open Heart Is Full of Love.

The Open Heart Brings Fulfillment.

The Open Heart Brings Bliss.

When Love Is Exchanged
Between Two Individuals
the Open Heart Brings Bliss.

The Open Heart Aids Others
to Open Their Hearts.

The Open Hearted One
Is a Powerful Resonator That
Lifts the Minds and Hearts
of Millions.

The Open Hearted One
Knows How to Build
Permanent Understandings
of Self and Creation.
The Open Hearted One
Knows How to Build
Permanent Understandings
of Self and Creation
at an Accelerated Rate.

The Open Heart Knows the Light.

The Open Heart Knows the Love.

The Open Heart Knows

the Present Moment.

The Still Mind
Enables the Open Heart to
Magnify its Power.

The Open Heart
Is the Gateway to the
Sacred Heart.

The Sacred Heart
Holds Within It the Core,
the Essence of One's Being.

Within the Open Heart

Is the Sacred Heart.

Within the Sacred Heart is Space.

Within This Space Is Love.

Love Is the Energy of Space.

All Life Enjoys Space.

Love and the Heart Are
Intimately Connected.

Love Lives in the Space
in the Heart.
Love Exists in the Space
in the Heart.
Love Is in the Space
in the Heart.

When Love Enters the
Space in the Heart the
Tension Dissipates.

Love in the Space in the
Sacred Heart Brings Peace.
Love in the Space in the
Sacred Heart Brings
World Peace.

Let the One of the Open Heart

Share this Universal Love with

All Who Would Receive.

The Open Heart Is the
Key to World Peace.
The Love of the Open Heart
Brings Peace to All.

Within Each Particle of Love
Lies the Communication Code
that Connects One With the
Entire Universe, the Sun,
the Planets, the Stars,
the Moon, and the
Inner Levels of
Consciousness.

Only the True One
Can Know Love.
Only the One of Love
Can Know Truth.

The One Who Knows Both
Knows Light and therefore,
En-light-en-ment.

The Most Enlightened Beings

Are also the Most

Love Filled.

The Heart Master Knows Love
Because the Heart Master
Knows the Heart.

Why Would Anyone Want

an Open heart?

To Receive the Love of the Universe.

To Receive the Love of Creation.

To Receive the Love of the All.

To Receive the Love of the Undivided.

To Receive One's True Essence as Love.

To Receive the Undivided.

Love Is at the Core of Everything.

The Open Heart Enables One

to Know Love.

Fear Closes the Heart.

Fear Closes the Heart to Love

and therefore to Knowing

the True Reality.

Love Binds Everything Together.

Where There Is Love

All Is Well.

Where Love Is Absent

Trouble Ensues.

The Open Heart Enables One

to Receive Love.

In Love There Is no Separation.

In the Open Heart

There Is no Separation.

All of Creation is One Unified
Substance and Being.
Knowing this Substance as Love
Enables One to Know and
Experience the Unified Whole.
The Open Heart Enables One
to fully Know Love and
therefore the Unified Whole.

In the Cave of the Heart
the Real Self Lives.
In the Cave of the Heart Is
the Burning Bush that Burns
Yet Fire Does Not Consume.

In the Cave of the Heart

Is I AM.

In the Cave of the Heart

Is the Burning Bush that

Gives Awareness of

I AM That I AM.

The Open Heart Practiced
Diligently and Consistently
Brings Forth the Large Golden
Ball of Light From the Heart.

The Open Heart Practiced
With the Full Commitment
of Discipline, Service and
Teaching Brings forth the Large
Golden-Pink-Shaft-Tube of Light
That Fully Connects With the
Love in Other's Hearts.

Only the Open Heart

Knows the Highest Love.

Only the Sacred Heart

Knows Real Love.

Only the One With the
Fire in the Heart Knows
How to Ignite the Fire
in Others' Hearts.

Only the Cave With the Fire
in the Heart Can Light Up
the Whole Body.

Only the One With the Fire

in the Heart Can Ignite the

Energy Above the Head.

Light Is Only Possible When
Love Is Fully Ignited in the
Fire of the Heart.
Truth, the Highest Truth,
Is Known by the
Fire in the Heart.
It Is by Fire That the
Open Heart Becomes Sacred.

The Fire in the Open,
Sacred Heart Makes
Everything Possible.
The One Who Ignites the
Fire of Life Becomes
the Initiator of Life.

What Is Life Without Light?

The Fire Brings Light.

The Fire in the Heart Brings

Full and Complete Understandings

and Awareness.

Who Is the Fire Hearted One?

The One of Light.

Who Is the Open Hearted One?

The One of Love.

Who Is the Sacred Hearted One?

The One of Truth.

Who Is the One Who Connects the
Heart with Other's Hearts?
The One of Compassion.

Who Is the One Who Connects the
Heart With the Whole World?
The One of Bliss, the World Server.

Who Is the One Who
Connects the Heart With the
Single Eye and the Crown?
The World Teacher.

What Is the One Who Connects the Heart

With Beyond the Crown?

Awake.

Being

Anyone who reads these pages and applies these Truths can gain a richer understanding and perspective of life.

Truth is usually simple. Yet, to know the greater and deeper Truths of Life requires diligent and consistent effort.

People tend to think in terms of the future and the past. Yet the True Reality is The Ever Present Now. We experience incomplete memories of the past and fantasies about the future, yet, the true, real, time and place for success and fulfillment is in the present moment.

In order to know the present moment each person must discipline the mind until the still mind is achieved. The stillness of mind enables one to know the still, present moment.

Thinking many thoughts with a busy brain will never enable one to know the True Reality. This is because most brain thoughts are generated from memories of sensory experiences.

Original thoughts rarely, if ever come from the brain. Original, great and high consciousness thoughts come from a mind; a still and quiet mind to be exact.

When the mind is quiet and still, it is like a blank blackboard. On this still, quiet, blank blackboard of the mind is written the messages from higher consciousness, Superconscious mind, and I AM.

Once the disciplined and still mind overrides and replaces the busy brain as the center of thought, then does the True Reality begin to be known.

In the present moment and still mind the Real Self also begins to be known. At this point the illusion begins to fall away.

What is this great illusion? This illusion is twofold.

1. The first part of the illusion is believing that the view of reality as given by the five physical senses is the total or accurate view of reality.

2. The second part of the illusion is in thinking that the physical environment is permanent, unchanging and lasting, and thinking that everything is separate from everything else.

In regards to the first part of the illusion our five physical senses of sight, smell, taste, touch and sound give us only a small portion of the total wavelength of physical reality, not to mention the realities of the subconscious and superconscious minds.

The light wavelength in the physical world stretches from the infrared to the ultraviolet. In between are, in addition to those wavelengths we perceive with the five physical senses, the wavelengths of radio waves, x-rays, gamma rays and much more.

In regards to the second part of the great illusion, the nature of the physical world is change. Everything is born, grows, contracts and then dies. Death is the withdrawal of energy life force and attention from the physical world.

If people find an experience to be pleasurable they want it to continue forever. When they have an unpleasurable or painful experience they seem to dwell on it forever or at least until the end of a lifetime.

People tend to be surprised or shocked over and over when things change in their environment. Yet, the nature of physical life is change.

These two great illusions have a name in the languages of India. This word is Maya.

Everything in the physical world is made up of a bunch of swirling atoms. Conglomerations of these atoms tend to give the illusion of stableness or solidity that we call physical matter, substance and form.

People confuse these changing, swirling, conglomerations of energy for something permanent, lasting, and unchangeable. This is why they are shocked or surprised when physical situations and circumstances change sometimes quickly, sometimes over time.

The still mind enables us to perceive reality as it is. The still mind enables us to know truth.

In the still mind each person develops and has the capacity to know, give and receive love on a much deeper level than the brain engrossed person. This is why the Open Heart follows the Still Mind and awareness of the Present Moment.

One has to have awareness of the mind to experience the Open Heart.

One has to be in the mind to begin to know the Open Heart.

One has to experience and be in the Present Moment to know the Open Heart.

The Open Heart is in The Stillness of The Present Moment.

About the Author

Throughout this lifetime, Daniel R. Condron has strived to understand the secrets of life and to explain them in a form that is understandable to all. He first experienced this as a young boy when he attained a connectedness with nature being in the woods and pastures while growing up on the family farm in northwest Missouri.

One day as a boy walking in the woods, Daniel sat down with his back against a giant white oak tree on the top of a hill. Daniel perceived, experienced, and saw the energy of the oak tree entering his body through his back. The energy moved up and down his spine and throughout the energy system-meridians of his back.

At other times while playing as a child in the family yard, his parents would notice Daniel gazing completely still, his body becoming completely motionless while standing as he received from the inner levels of consciousness.

At other times, he noticed he could not take his attention off his breath, showing he came into this lifetime already having mastered pranayama. As a child, Daniel became frustrated at this because he wanted his attention freed in order to go play with the other children.

Daniel's first conscious meditation came on a cool autumn day. The young boy, Daniel, laid down in a ditch between two hills that was filled with three-feet-deep fallen leaves. Being completely relaxed and looking up at the blue sky his mind became still.

Daniel also received life force energy from the rows of 50-foot-tall Bois-de'Arc hedge trees as he ran through the quarter mile tunnel made by their overhanging branches.

In the year 2000, Daniel opened all seven energy centers–chakras and experienced bliss.

In the year 2006, Daniel opened his 8th and 9th chakras and experienced an even higher bliss of consciousness and being.

He has devoted his life to gaining and receiving the full enlightenment through discipline, service and teaching in order to know the Real Self, what is permanent and lasting, Eternal and the True Reality.

This he teaches to others through the understanding of the Still Mind, the Present Moment, and the Open Heart.

He resides with his wife Barbara and son Hezekiah on the 1,500 acre College of Metaphysics campus near Springfield, Missouri.

Why Practice the Still Mind?

1. The Still Mind is more efficient than a busy brain.

2. The still Mind enables Self to receive from subconscious mind.

3. The Still Mind enables one to receive from superconscious mind.

4. The Still Mind enables one to know I AM.

5. The Still Mind enables one to receive and be filled with Light.

6. The Still Mind enables one to succeed.

7. The Still Mind enables the greatest and Highest success.

8. The Still Mind heals.

9. The Still Mind brings peace.

10. The Still Mind relieves stress.

11. The Still Mind enables Self to know the Present Moment which is the True Reality.

12. The Still Mind leads to the Present Moment which leads to the Open Heart. The Open Heart is the doorway to the Sacred Heart which brings the highest love into the world.

13. The Still Mind brings awareness of connectedness with all and interconnectedness with the ALL.

Other titles by Dr. Daniel R. Condron

The Emptiness Sutra

The Secret Code of Revelation

The Purpose of Life

The Tao Te Ching Interpreted and Explained

Permanent Healing

Superconscious Meditation:
    Kundalini & the Understanding
    of the Whole Mind

Dreams of the Soul: The Yogi Sutras of Pantanjali

The Universal Language of Mind—
    The Book of Matthew Interpreted

Understanding Your Dreams

The Four Stages of Growth

The Seven Keys to Prosperity and Abundance

Isaiah 55: Interpreted and Explained

Additional titles available from SOM Publishing include:

The Moon's Effect on Dreams by Dr. Christine Madar, ed.
ISBN: 0-944385-42-3 $10.00

Lucid Dreaming by Dr. Teresa Martin, ed.
ISBN: 0-944385-41-5 $12.00

The Law of Attraction by Dr. Laurel Clark
ISBN: 0-944385-39-3 $10.00

The Emptiness Sutra by Dr. Daniel R. Condron
ISBN: 0-944385-38-5 $10.00

The Secret Code of Revelation by Dr. Daniel R. Condron
ISBN: 0-944386-37-7 $15.00

The Purpose of Life by Dr. Daniel R. Condron
ISBN: 0-944386-35-0 $15.00

Master Living by Dr. Barbara Condron
ISBN: 0-944386-36-9 $18.00

Dharma: Finding Your Soul's Purpose by Dr. Laurel Clark
ISBN: 0-944386-34-2 $10.00

Every Dream is About the Dreamer
Dr. Barbara Condron
ISBN: 0-944386-27-X $13.00

**Peace Making: 9 Lessons for Changing Yourself, Your
Relationships, & the World** by Dr. Barbara Condron
ISBN: 0-944386-31-8 $12.00

The Tao Te Ching Interpreted & Explained
Dr. Daniel R. Condron
ISBN: 0-944385-30-x $15.00

How to Raise an Indigo Child by Dr. Barbara Condron
ISBN: 0-944386-29-6 $14.00

Karmic Healing by Dr. Laurel Clark
ISBN: 0-944386-26-1 $15.00

Spiritual Renaissance: Elevating Your Consciousness for the Common Good by Dr. Barbara Condron
ISBN: 0-944386-22-9 $15.00

Permanent Healing by Dr. Daniel Condron
ISBN: 0-944386-12-1 $13.00

Superconscious Meditation: Kundalini & Understanding the Whole Mind by Dr. Daniel R. Condron
ISBN: 0-944386-21-0 $13.00

First Opinion: Wholistic Health Care in the 21st Century
Dr. Barbara Condron
ISBN: 0-944386-18-0 $15.00

The Dreamer's Dictionary by Dr. Barbara Condron
ISBN: 0-944386-16-4 $15.00

The Work of the Soul by Dr. Barbara Condron, ed.
ISBN: 0-944386-17-2 $13.00

Uncommon Knowledge: Past Life & Health Readings
Dr. Barbara Condron, ed.
ISBN: 0-944386-19-9 $13.00

The Universal Language of Mind: The Book of Matthew Interpreted by Dr. Daniel R. Condron
ISBN: 0-944386-15-6 $13.00

Dreams of the Soul: The Yogi Sutras of Pantanjali
Dr. Daniel R. Condron
ISBN: 0-944386-11-3 $13.00

Kundalini Rising: Mastering Your Creative Energies
Dr. Barbara Condron
ISBN: 0-944386-13-X $13.00

To order write:

School of Metaphysics
World Headquarters
163 Moon Valley Road
Windyville, Missouri 65783 U.S.A.

Enclose a check or money order payable in U.S. funds to SOM with any order. Please include $5.00 for postage and handling of books, $10.00 for international orders.

For those who would like to study and learn the teachings in this book and desire to grow in awareness and uplift their consciousness coursework is available.

A complete catalogue of all book titles, audio lectures and courses, and videos is available upon request.

Visit us on the Internet at www.som.org
email: som@som.org